Tabatha lives on Hayling Island in Hampshire. She is
married to Richard and has two children, Tegan and Jonny,
who are the inspiration for this book.

Tabatha has enjoyed writing poetry from a young age but
had no thoughts of getting her work published until now.
She is hoping to have more work published in the future. Her
hobbies include music, yoga and time with her family.

Nanny Can't Remember

TABATHA THROUP

Illustrated by Sue Martin

AUSTIN MACAULEY PUBLISHERS™

LONDON • CAMBRIDGE • NEW YORK • SHARJAH

A CIP catalogue record for this title is available from the British Library.

ISBN 9781788783064 (Paperback)
ISBN 9781788783071 (E-Book)

www.austinmacauley.com

First Published (2019)
Austin Macauley Publishers Ltd
25 Canada Square
Canary Wharf
London
E14 5LQ

This book is dedicated to my parents Pam and Colin Brown. Pam for being an outgoing and vibrant mother for so many years and Colin for being so patient and caring towards all of us.

Gratitude to Sue Martin for all the lovely Illustrations
she created for my book.

Nanny has always been special and sweet
She played fun games and gave us treats
But lately she has changed a bit

She gives less cuddles and gets in a muddle
Sometimes she seems sad or cross
But Mummy says it's not her fault.

"Are you on your holidays?"
"No, Nanny, it's September."
Mummy says we must be kind
Because Nanny can't remember.

New Year's Eve was lots of fun
Nanny and Grandad decided to come
We danced to music from their time
Nanny seemed like she was on cloud nine
Jumping and clapping and smiling, and so
That memory for us will never go.

"Is it nearly Summer?"
"No, Nanny, it's December."
Please remember to be kind
Because Nanny can't remember.

Nanny and Grandad came for Sunday roast
It's the day they seem to like the most
They talk about their days gone by
With a cheeky grin and a glint in the eye
It's nice to see them laugh like this
One day, it's something we will miss.

"Are we going home now, Bill?"
It sounds like she's in a temper
We must remember to be kind
Cos Nanny can't remember.

Grandad finds it rather tough
But if you love someone, it is enough
You're there for them
Through thick and thin
With all the challenges
That life can bring.

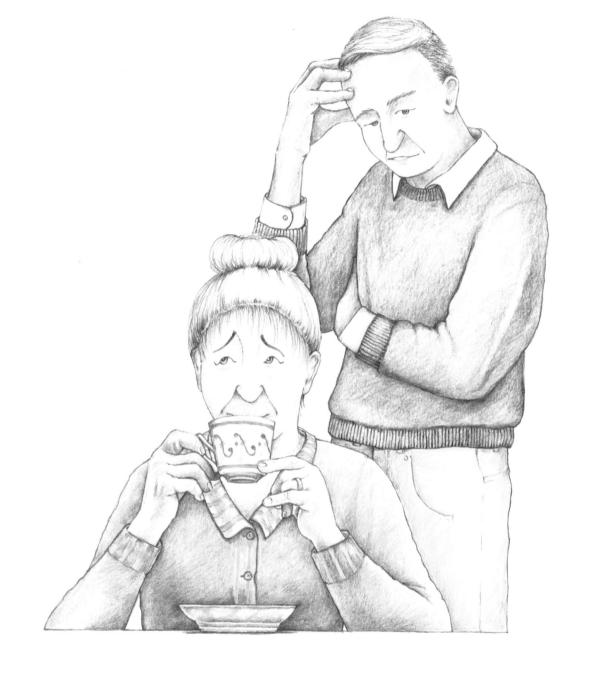

Nanny's memory will soon get worse
But we never would offend her
Always promise to be kind
When someone has dementia.